Christmas Program Builder
No. 48

Resources for Christmas Programs
*Recitations * Monologues * Sketches*

Compiled by Paul Miller

Unless otherwise indicated, Scripture quotations are from the *Holy Bible, New International Version®* (NIV®). Copyright © 1973, 1978, 1984 by International Bible Society. Used by permission of Zondervan Publishing House. All rights reserved.

Lillenas PUBLISHING COMPANY
KANSAS CITY, MO 64141

Contents

Recitations

Little Angels

(For ages 3-5. One child or several children in a row, dressed as angels, followed by a song.)

ALL: We are just little angels;
      We have not been here long.
      But we want to worship Jesus,
      So please listen to our song!
          —Enelle Eder

Happy Birthday, Little King

(For ages 3-5. May be used with "Little Angels" above. Sung to the tune of "Jesus Loves Me.")

Happy birthday, little King.
You are why we clap and sing.
Christmas tells us of Your birth;
We are glad You came to earth!

We love You, Jesus!
We love You, Jesus!
We love You, Jesus!
You are the King of Kings!
          —Enelle Eder

The King's Birthday

(For ages 3-5. May be used with "Little Angels" above. Sung to the tune of "Away in a Manger.")

In Bethlehem town, a long time ago,
A baby was born, God's love to show.
The shepherds all worshiped; the angels did sing,
For it was the birthday of Jesus the King!
          —Enelle Eder

Baby Jesus

(May be recited by one or divided for three children)

Baby Jesus, tiny and dear,
Placed in a manger with animals near.

Baby Jesus, the Son of God,
Visited by shepherds with staff and rod.

Baby Jesus, so sweet and pure,
Wise men gave Him gold, frankincense, and myrrh.
          —Wanda E. Brunstetter

To Each of You

CHILD 1: We've tried our best to please you

CHILD 2: In all the things we've done;

CHILD 3: We've tried to speak of Jesus,

CHILD 4: Our dear God's only Son.

CHILD 5: We hope you have been pleased

CHILD 6: And enjoyed the program too;

ALL: Now *(pause),* merry, merry Christmas

To each one of you!
          —Helen Kitchell Evans

Wondrous Star

CHILD 1: Star light,

CHILD 2: Star bright,

CHILD 3: You gave out the news that night.

CHILD 4: Shining there so high

CHILD 5: In Bethlehem's dark sky.

CHILD 6: Wondrous star, you gave to earth

CHILD 7: The news of Jesus' birth.

CHILD 1: Star light!

CHILD 2: Star bright!

ALL: Blessed star that shone that night.
                    —*Helen Kitchell Evans*

That's What We Call Christmas

CHILD 1: Family time with relations,

CHILD 2: Get together in all nations,

ALL: That's what we call Christmas.

CHILD 3: Special cookies, special cakes,

CHILD 4: All good things that Mother bakes,

ALL: That's what we call Christmas.

CHILD 5: Presents underneath the tree,

CHILD 6: Some for all the family,

ALL: That's what we call Christmas.

CHILD 7: Everyone on knees to pray

CHILD 8: On this very special day,

ALL: That's what we call Christmas.

CHILD 9: Worshiping with friends and others,

CHILD 10: These we call our Christian brothers,

ALL: That's what we call Christmas.
                    —*Helen Kitchell Evans*

When Christmas Day Is Here

CHILD 1: No matter how bad the weather,

CHILD 2: It doesn't matter whether

CHILD 3: We have ice or snow

CHILD 4: We're always ready to go

ALL: When Christmas Day is here!

CHILD 1: We're always ready to celebrate

CHILD 2: When it comes that special date,

CHILD 3: The day our Savior came to earth,

CHILD 4: It's the day of dear Jesus' birth.

ALL: When Christmas Day is here!

CHILD 1: So gather all the family,

CHILD 2: Fill your hearts with joy and glee;

CHILD 3: Worship at home and church with love;

CHILD 4: Pray to the Father up above.

ALL: When Christmastime is here!
                    —*Helen Kitchell Evans*

What Joy!

CHILD 1: What joy the bright star
gave
To all upon the earth.

CHILD 2: What joy when Christ arrived
We bless His holy birth.

CHILD 3: Angels spoke to shepherds
And they traveled to see the
King.

CHILD 4: Wise men rode to Bethlehem
Their precious gifts to bring.

CHILD 5: Mary loved her baby
Sent from heaven above.

CHILD 6: Jesus grew to be a man
To all He showed great love.

ALL: Wonderful days of Christmas;
Wonderful days of joy!
Bless this holy infant;
Mary's baby boy!
—*Helen Kitchell Evans*

A Christian Every Day

I'm a Christian on this Christmas
I try to be each day;
I am kind to others, and—*(Pause)*
I watch what I say! *(Leaves quickly)*
—*Helen Kitchell Evans*

Jesus, Our Friend

CHILD 1: We sing because we are
happy.

CHILD 2: We sing because He came.

CHILD 3: We sing of our dear Jesus.

ALL: We sing to bless His name.

All *(sing to the tune of "Mary Had a
Little Lamb"):*
Jesus is our dearest friend,
Dearest friend, dearest friend;
Jesus is our dearest friend
We sing to bless His name.

Jesus loves us very much,
Very much, very much;
Jesus loves us very much
We bless His holy name.
—*Helen Kitchell Evans*

A Little Afraid

I'm a little afraid
What shall I say?
Except wish you all
A happy Jesus day!
—*Robert Colbert*

The Christmas Stars

*(Each child should carry a large yellow
star with a picture in the center, appropriate to what they are speaking about.)*

CHILD 1: Come see in the star brave
Joseph of old,
Who traveled to Bethlehem
as he was told.

CHILD 2: Come see in the star young
Mary so fair;
She laid her sweet baby in
the manger there.

CHILD 3: Come see in the star the Baby so dear;
He slept without sound with
animals near.

CHILD 4: Come see in the star shepherds at night,
Led to Bethlehem by God's
own light.

CHILD 5: Come see in the star bright
angels above,
Bringing the message of
peace and love.

CHILD 6: Come see the wise men
from lands afar;
They found the Child be-
neath the star.

CHILD 7: Come see below the star a
stable dim,
Where many came to wor-
ship Him.

ALL: Come see all the stars in the
Christmas sky,
Twinkling the message of
One from on high.
—Enelle Eder

Each Heart

Christmas is a time
For Christ to be born
In each heart,
To become our King,
Savior, and Lord.
—Robert Colbert

The Father's Gift

We give our thanks
This Christmas morn
Because our Lord
And King is born.

He brought to earth
His peace and love;
The Father's gift
From heaven above.
—Robert Colbert

In Bethlehem

In Bethlehem
A king is born,
Shepherds and angels say.
O come, let's hasten
To worship Him,
This blessed Christmas Day!
—Robert Colbert

Ask Me

Ask me about Christmas,
And here's what I'll say,
"It's the day
That Christ was born";
Did I do OK?
—Robert Colbert

You Are Welcome

My joy this Christmas
Has no bounds,
Because I just love
Having you around!
Welcome! Welcome! Welcome!
—Evangeline Carey

God Sent His Son!

God sent His Son,
The Baby Jesus is born;
And I'm so glad He came
On that Christmas morn!
—Evangeline Carey

God's Love!

God's love
Warms through and through;
It brings Christmas blessings today,
And all the New Year too!
—Evangeline Carey

May You Share the Blessings of Christmas!

Christmas brings so much happiness,
  Especially today;
Christmas brings family and friends,
  Blessings in every way!
            —*Evangeline Carey*

Have a Blessed Holiday

May your holiday be filled
With just what you need,
Because there's so much love
Given and received!
            —*Evangeline Carey*

My Christmas Wish!

This Christmas wish
  Is packed with love,
And prayers that you'll be blessed
By our Lord up above!
            —*Evangeline Carey*

What Makes It Special?

What makes Christmas Day so special?
  Jesus came to earth to say,
"Follow my Father in heaven,
  And you'll live in heaven someday."
            —*Helen Kitchell Evans*

My Special Teddy Bear

My teddy bear is special,
So I brought him along.
He isn't going to sing;
He doesn't know any song.

But he can wave his paw,
  And I know what he'd like to say:
Have a wonderful time
  When it is Christmas Day. *(Wave bear's paw.)*
            —*Helen Kitchell Evans*

Without Fame

I'm quite small
  And without fame,
But all of you
  Know my name.

I'm here to tell
  A great big story
About the King
  And all His glory.

He was born at Christmas
  Many years ago;
Our Savior, our King;
  We all love Him so.
            —*Helen Kitchell Evans*

Gifts of Love

What am I giving for Christmas?
  I'm giving the gift of love—
The gift that costs me nothing;
  It was sent from heaven above.

When the package of love arrived,
  There was more than enough, you see.
So what am I giving for Christmas?
  The love that was given to me.
            —*Helen Kitchell Evans*

No End

CHILD 1: On Christmas Jesus came to
us,
Our Savior and our
Friend;
His blessings we receive
each day,
Of them there is no end.

CHILD 2: He gives us courage, gives
us faith,
And wisdom for each task;
His power is there for every-
one,
We only need to ask.

CHILD 3: Through prayer He walks
with each of us
Upon this Christmas Day;
Let's take His hand and let
Him lead
The truly Christian way.
—*Helen Kitchell Evans*

We Can Worship Jesus

CHILD 1: The wise men traveled from
afar
And brought their gifts so
rare.
They bowed before the
Christ child
And paid Him homage
there.

CHILD 2: Though we didn't travel
with them
Or see the shining star,
We all can worship Jesus
No matter where we are.
—*Roma Joy Smith*

I Bring

*(A presentation for eight children, ages 6-
10. Each child enters holding a large,
wrapped box with the appropriate word
displayed on the front. After each line,
the child puts the box on the floor, ar-
ranging them in a pyramid or other
shape for display.)*

FIRST: I bring my gift of TIME
In honor of His birth.
I will try to use it wisely
While I am here on
earth.

SECOND: I bring my gift of TAL-
ENTS,
Whatever they may be.
I will use them for His glory
Because He gave them just
to me!

THIRD: I bring the gift of WOR-
SHIP
For the Savior I adore.
May His sweet and holy
presence
Fill my heart forever-
more.

FOURTH: I bring the gift of
PRAYER,
For this is the way I
know
To talk to Jesus daily
So He will guide me as I
go.

FIFTH: I bring the gift of STUDY;
I'll grow by reading His
Word.
And when He speaks to
me,
His voice will surely be
heard.

SIXTH: I bring the gift of PRAISE.
My lips should always
tell

How much I love the Sav-
ior,
And in my heart He'll
dwell.

SEVENTH: I bring my gift of
THANKS
To God for sending His
Son.
I will remember to give
Him glory,
For He is the Chosen
One.

EIGHTH: I bring my gift of LOVE,
Not just at this Christmas
season.
But I will show my love all
year,
And Jesus is the reason.

ALL: Jesus, we bring these gifts
To show our love to You,
Not just at Christmastime,
But all the year-long
through!
—*Enelle Eder*

It's Christmas

(For one child or three)

The air is nippy;
The ground is white
While we sing carols
This Christmas night.

The stockings are hung
All in a row.
The gifts are wrapped
And the candles glow.

The story is read
Of Jesus' birth,
And we thank the Lord
He came to earth.
—*Margaret Primrose*

Jesus Is God's Promise

Jesus is God's Promise
Pledged so long ago,
So we could have deliverance
From sin with all its woe.

His birth in lowly Bethlehem
Was proof God keeps His word.
Yes, as a helpless baby
God came—our precious Lord.
—*Roma Joy Smith*

It's Nice

It is nice to come to Sunday School
And join with those we love
In singing and in worship
Of our dear Savior up above.

So at this happy Christmastime
Let's hear those voices ring
With praise and hallelujah
To our Savior and our King.

(Follow this with adult and children's chorus combined singing the "Hallelujah Chorus.")
—*Helen Kitchell Evans*

Wintertime Is Special

I'll tell you why I like winter,
It's the fun time of the year;
Snowfall, sleds, and Christmas,
Everything brings cheer.

It's the birthday of our Savior.
To Him we give our praise;
That's why winter is so special
In so many different ways.
—*Helen Kitchell Evans*

Wasn't It Wonderful?

CHILD 1: Wasn't it wonderful when
Jesus came
That all was quiet and
still
In that lowly stable?
Time seemed to stand
still.

CHILD 2: All was quiet, except now
and then
There was a baby's cry;
Then the voices of the animals
Standing in stalls close
by.

CHILD 3: Wasn't it wonderful God
loved us
So very much upon this
earth
That He sent the holy angels
To sing of this great
birth?

CHILD 4: Yes, the greatness of that
special day
Will last as long as the
stars that shine;
Jesus, our Lord, sent to us
To forgive your sins—and
mine.

ALL: Wasn't it wonderful that Je-
sus came?
How great is our God
above!
Oh, the wonderful blessing
He gives us!
Oh, how great must be
His love!
—Helen Kitchell Evans

Praise to Him

All people have a birthday;
It's a very outstanding day.
And everyone celebrates
In their own happy way.

Christmas is Jesus' birthday,
Celebrated over all the earth,
For our Savior was born in a stable
And the world knows of His birth.

His coming was extraspecial
For He was God's only Son
Sent from heaven to us
To save each and every one.

Every year we celebrate
The birthday of our King;
We gather together as Christians
To give praise to Him and sing.
—Helen Kitchell Evans

Christ Has Come to Earth

Come, children, now of every race
Of every color, creed;
Praise God who loves all very much
And cares for every need.

From every land upon the earth
Gather to His side;
Let all the world hear you say
That in His love you abide.

From every hilltop let voices ring
The praises of His birth;
Let every song be one of joy,
For Christ has come to earth.

*(Follow with a spirited song by the chil-
dren's choir.)*

—Helen Kitchell Evans

Spelling Christmas

(Each child enters holding a letter. When finished, they all spell out "Christmas.")

C is for the Christ child
　　Born upon that day.
He came to be our Savior—
　　The Truth, the Life, the Way.

H is for the herald angels
　　Singing in the night.
Filling evening skies
　　With His holy light.

R means our Redeemer
　　Came to bring the light.
In a world of darkness,
　　His message shines so bright.

I stands for Israel,
　　Land of Bethlehem town;
And in a lowly stable
　　The glory of heaven came down.

S is for the star
　　That shone so bright.
Telling of Jesus' birth
　　That first Christmas night.

T is for three wise men,
　　They who traveled far
In search of Baby Jesus,
　　Guided by the star.

M is for the manger
　　Where Baby Jesus lay,
Sleeping peacefully
　　On a bed of hay.

A is for all He stands for:
　　Savior, and Healer of men,
The great Baptizer, and
　　The King who's coming again.

S means shepherds came
　　To the stable dim.
And fell upon their knees
　　To praise and worship Him.

ALL: Merry Christmas!
—Enelle Eder

Favorite Place

My favorite place is in Sunday
　　School
Where I learn about the Golden Rule;
Where I hear the stories of Jesus, my
　　King,
And with other children sing and
　　sing.

Sunday School when it's Christmas-
　　time,
Sunday School every Sunday
Makes me a better Christian
When I go to the other school on
　　Monday.
—Helen Kitchell Evans

Favorite Season

Christmas is such a happy time;
　　It's my favorite season.
It's the birthday of our Jesus;
　　I'm sure that is my reason.

Christmas is a time of giving,
　　A time of special sharing,
A time for love for others,
　　A time for really caring.

Christmas is old, yet ever new.
　　Each year is never the same;
We feel an extraspecial love
　　When we think how Jesus came.
—Helen Kitchell Evans

God's Gift

There is a gift we get each day
  Of which none can compare;
A gift that came to us from heaven,
  God's tender love and constant care.

The gift of Baby Jesus came;
  The story we all know.
Today that gift follows us
  Everywhere we go.

This gift is the reason for our joy
  Each day upon this earth;
We all rejoice at Christmastime,
  For it's the day of Jesus' birth.
        —*Helen Kitchell Evans*

The Christ Child

Each time we hear the story
  It's old, yet ever new.
How the Christ child came to earth,
  Bringing love and mercy to me and
  you!

He was born of the Virgin Mary;
  Angels announced His holy birth.
There in the stable where cattle fed,
  A shining light glowed round His
  head.

Shepherds hastened to Bethlehem,
  Leaving their flock that night.
They felt the glory of His presence
  And gazed at the heavens bright.

They found the Babe with Joseph and
  Mary—
  Out there in the lowly stall.
God had sent the Blessed Redeemer
  To bear the sins of one and all!
        —*Lorene Beeler*

Christmas

It isn't the ribbons,
  The trimmings, and trappings.
It's the love of family and friends
  That make the glad wrappings.

It isn't the glitter
  Of tinsel bright.
It's the warmth of a Child
  On a starless night.

It isn't the sound
  Of tinkling bells.
It's the silence in the heart
  Where *His* spirit dwells!
        —*Lorene Beeler*

Three Christmas Gifts

One king gave Him gold
  As he journeyed from afar.
He was led to the stable
  By rays of a white, brilliant star.

One king brought sweet incense
  To lay at the Babe's feet.
Angels tenderly hovered near
  Making the scene complete!

The third king gave myrrh
  And knelt to worship Him.
In hearts of truth and love
  His star will never dim.
        —*Lorene Beeler*

Thank God for the Gift

Thank God for the gift of His Son;
He's given us more than we deserve.
Thank God for His mercy
And for being true to His Word!
—*Evangeline Carey*

Newborn Lord

A bright, shiny star
Glows in my heart,
Because I worship
The newborn Lord.

No silver or gold
To Him I bring,
Just humble praise
For Christ our King.
—*Robert Colbert*

King of Glory

Christ is our King of glory;
He is our Lord of Lords.
Come, let's welcome Him
Today into our hearts.
Come with joyful praises;
God's great love divine
Comes to bless us all
At this happy Christmastime!
—*Robert Colbert*

His Love and Care

We give gifts all the year,
But at Christmas they seem extra
great;
That's because of Jesus' birth;
That's a wonderful date.

Jesus, who came to bring love
For each of us to share;
Let's give thanks this Christmastime
For all His love and care.
—*Helen Kitchell Evans*

Could This Be the King?

The brilliant star moved slowly
That the wise men might see the
way
As they traveled on to Bethlehem
To the place where Jesus lay.

And as the camels plodded on
Expectations of joy mounted high,
For soon they would face the King
That prophets foretold in days gone
by.

They found Him in a manger;
Around Him lowing cattle milled.
Could this be the King so prophe-
sied?
Could this be the promise fulfilled?
—*Helen Kitchell Evans*

The Savior Is Here

Bethlehem's cradle and Calvary's
cross
Merged on Christmas Day;
Our redemption unfolded here
Where a baby slept on a bed of hay.

The Savior arrived for the hopeless,
For lost people everywhere;
Many rejoiced and gave thanks
For the wonderful news heard
there.

Let us rejoice anew this season
As the birth of our Savior draws
near;
Let us share the "Good News" with
others—
The Savior at last is here!
—*Helen Kitchell Evans*

A Shepherd Boy's Christmas

I'm sitting on a hillside;
    Nearby, our resting sheep.
The night is dark and lonely;
    I'm trying not to sleep.

My father is a shepherd;
    I'm here with him tonight.
The herdsmen talk to pass the time.
    Oh! *(Gasps)* What was that bright
    light?

An angel speaks, "Don't be afraid.
    To you good news I bring—
A child's been born in Bethlehem.
    'Tis Christ, the Lord and King.

"You'll find Him in a stable
    Amid the dust and hay.
He's lying in a manger.
    The inns were full today."

And now a choir of angels
    Is giving praise to God.
My father's hands are trembling.
    He drops his shepherd's rod.

The angels leave for heaven;
    We're running to the stall
To see the Baby Jesus,
    Who came to save us all.
        —*Margaret Primrose*

Juan's Christmas

"¡Buenos días!"

That's what I say to people
    When you would just say, "Hi."
I said it to a tourist
    When she was passing by.

She stopped to buy bananas
    From stacks upon the ground,
Then chose the biggest oranges
    From Mother's little mound.

"What's on your list for Christmas?"
    She asked me with a smile.
At first I couldn't tell her.
    I had to think a while.

"I'd like a bag of popcorn,"
    I said so she could hear.
She handed me this peso
    And wiped away a tear.
(Pause)

I wonder why she cried.
        —*Margaret Primrose*

Plays, Monologues, and Programs

Responsive Readings for Advent and Christmas

by Keith Schwanz

Down and Dirty

PASTOR: Jesus, the Word, was with God before the beginning. Jesus, the Son of God, flung the galaxies into orbit at the creation. Jesus, the Son of Man, voluntarily accepted the limitations of time and space in order to reveal the very essence of God.

Dust bathed Jesus' feet as He walked the dirt paths of Galilee. He battled hunger and thirst and fatigue. Jesus asked His Father to deliver Him from death, the most bitter of human experiences, but He was crucified and buried only to emerge from the tomb as the victorious Lord. Jesus, the royal Ruler of all things, came down from glory and lived in our dirty world.

MEN: Jesus, who being in very nature God, did not consider equality with God something to be grasped.

WOMEN: This is how the birth of Jesus Christ came about. His mother Mary was pledged to be married to Joseph, but before they came together, she was found to be with child through the Holy Spirit.

MEN: Jesus made himself nothing, taking the very nature of a servant, being made in human likeness.

WOMEN: An angel of the Lord appeared to Joseph in a dream and said, "Joseph son of David, do not be afraid to take Mary home as your wife, because what is conceived in her is from the Holy Spirit. She will give birth to a son . . ."

MEN: "And being found in appearance as a man, [Jesus] humbled himself and became obedient to death—even death on a cross!"

WOMEN: "' . . . You are to give him the name of Jesus, because he will save his people from their sins.' All this took place to fulfill what the Lord had said through the prophet: 'The virgin will be with child and will give birth to a son, and they will call him Immanuel'—which means, 'God with us.'"

MEN: "Therefore God exalted him to the highest place and gave him the name that is above every name,

CONGREGATION: "That at the name of Jesus every knee should bow, in heaven and on earth and under the earth, and every tongue confess that Jesus Christ is Lord, to the glory of God the Father."

PASTOR: Jesus experienced the full spectrum of what all of us face. He knows—intimately—the ups and downs of life on earth. The good news for us is that Jesus, the humble servant, will help every person who invites Him to be Savior and Lord.

O come to my heart, Lord Jesus.

CONGREGATION: There is room in my heart for You.

Just Ordinary Guys

PASTOR: They weren't anything special. They didn't have closets full of clothes. They didn't own the best house on the block. They were just ordinary guys working the night shift.

CONGREGATION: "There were shepherds living out in the fields nearby, keeping watch over their flocks at night."

PASTOR: They didn't enjoy the privileges of the social elite. Usually no one paid much attention to them. But on this night God focused the celestial spotlight on these common shepherds. At God's prompting, the shepherds stepped to center stage in the play of plays.

MEN: "An angel of the Lord appeared to them,

WOMEN: "And the glory of the Lord shone around them,

CONGREGATION: "And they were terrified.

CHOIR: "But the angel said to them,

WOMEN: "'Do not be afraid. I bring you good news of great joy that will be for all the people.

MEN: "'Today in the town of David a Savior has been born to you;

CONGREGATION: "'He is Christ the Lord.'"

PASTOR: Christ the Lord. This little baby was the Christ. He was a shepherd, too—the Good Shepherd. Jesus was the Savior sent by God to find sheep wandering in the night of sin.

CONGREGATION: "The Lord—Jesus—is our Shepherd. We shall lack nothing.

MEN: "He makes us to lie down in green pastures,

WOMEN: "He leads us beside still waters,

CONGREGATION: "He restores our souls. He guides us in the paths of righteousness for his name's sake."

CHOIR: The shepherds "spread the word concerning what had been told them about this child,

CONGREGATION: "And all who heard it were amazed at what the shepherds said to them."

PASTOR: Amazed! The people were amazed. Messiah had come, and the first to know it were just ordinary guys. They may have been ignored by most people in their society, but God didn't overlook them.

And God won't overlook you, either. God sent His Son so that you can have life—abundant and eternal—if you invite Him to be Savior and Lord.

O come to my heart, Lord Jesus.

CONGREGATION: There is room in my heart for You.

No Surprise

PASTOR: The birth of Jesus came as no surprise. An angelic messenger told Mary that she had been chosen to be the mother of Christ. She knew what was happening. Joseph had been instructed to name the baby Jesus. He knew what to expect. Centuries earlier, prophets spoke the word of God, telling us of the coming Messiah. They knew God's plan.
For to us a child is born,

MEN: "While they were there, the time came for the baby to be born,"

PASTOR: **to us a Son is given.**

WOMEN: "and she gave birth to her firstborn, a son. She wrapped him in cloths and placed him in a manger, because there was no room for them in the inn."

PASTOR: **And he will be called Wonderful Counselor.**

CONGREGATION: "I have told you these things, so that in me you may have peace."

CHOIR: "Do not let your hearts be troubled. Trust in God; trust also in me."

PASTOR: **He will be called . . . Mighty God.**

WOMEN: "They all asked, 'Are you then the Son of God?'

MEN: "[Jesus] replied, 'You are right in saying I am.'"

CONGREGATION: "All authority in heaven and on earth has been given to me."

PASTOR: **He will be called . . . Everlasting Father.**

MEN: "'I tell you the truth,' Jesus answered, 'before Abraham was born, I am!'"

WOMEN: "In the beginning was the Word, and the Word was with God, and the Word was God.

CONGREGATION: "He was with God in the beginning."

PASTOR: **He will be called . . . Prince of Peace.**

CHOIR: "[Jesus] got up and rebuked the winds and the waves, and it was completely calm.

MEN: "The men were amazed and asked, 'What kind of man is this?

CONGREGATION: "'Even the winds and the waves obey him!"

WOMEN: "'Be quiet!' Jesus said sternly. 'Come out of him!'

CONGREGATION: "The evil spirit shook the man violently and came out of him with a shriek.

CHOIR: "The people were so amazed that they asked each other, 'What is this? A new teaching—and with authority! He even gives orders to evil spirits and they obey him.'"

PASTOR: The birth of Jesus in your heart will not take you by surprise either. God has promised to abide with every person who invites Jesus to be Savior and Lord.

O come to my heart, Lord Jesus.

CONGREGATION: There is room in my heart for You.

Night Lights

PASTOR: The angels were busy in preparation for the first Christmas. God sent them winging between heaven and earth with the message that Messiah was coming. In a whisper so as not to frighten her, the angel told Mary the good news.

WOMEN: "Do not be afraid, Mary, you have found favor with God. You will be with child and give birth to a son, and you are to give him the name of Jesus. He will be great and will be called the Son of the Most High."

PASTOR: Mary rejoiced in God's blessing.

Joseph, however, thought the blessing was only a disgrace. To save Mary from public embarrassment, he made plans to quietly break their engagement. So God sent an angel with a message for Joseph.

MEN: "Joseph son of David, do not be afraid to take Mary home as your wife, because what is conceived in her is from the Holy Spirit. She will give birth to a son, and you are to give him the name Jesus, because he will save his people from their sins."

PASTOR: Joseph obeyed God's instructions.

On the night Jesus was born, shepherds cared for their sheep out on a Judean hillside. At God's command, an angel hurried to tell the shepherds that Messiah had come.

MEN: "I bring you good news of great joy that will be for all the people.

WOMEN: "Today in the town of David a Savior has been born to you;

CONGREGATION: "He is Christ the Lord.

MEN: "This will be a sign to you:

WOMEN: "You will find a baby wrapped in cloths and lying in a manger."

PASTOR: Suddenly, a multitude of angels leaped into the sky and illuminated the night with praise.

CONGREGATION: "Glory to God in the highest and on earth peace to men on whom his favor rests."

PASTOR: The shepherds hurried into town at the angels' prompting. The angels had been totally correct in their description of the Christ. The shepherds praised God for the miracle of the Messiah.

We don't need angelic night light in our dark world to bring messages of hope. God has spoken to us by His Son. Jesus, the Light of the World, brings the good news of God's love to every person who invites Him to be Savior and Lord.

O come to my heart, Lord Jesus.

CONGREGATION: There is room in my heart for You.

Jesus, the Christ

PASTOR: The Christ. Anointed One. Messiah. Prophets told Israel that God would send a Savior. Year after year they waited. With every birth in Bethlehem they asked, "Is this Messiah?" Finally, while Caesar Augustus ruled the Roman Empire and Quirinius was governor of Syria, angels announced the birth of the Christ to shepherds in a field.

WOMEN: "Today in the town of David a Savior has been born to you; he is Christ the Lord."

MEN: The shepherds hurried off and found the Baby. They returned to their flocks, glorifying and praising God for all the things they had heard and seen. They had seen Messiah.

PASTOR: For 30 years, "Jesus grew in wisdom and stature, and in favor with God and men." At the appointed hour, Jesus began to preach the good news as the Anointed One of God. Many heard Jesus speak and believed. One of the first was Andrew, who hurried to tell his brother about Messiah.

MEN: After spending the day with Jesus, the first thing Andrew did was to find his brother Simon and tell him, "'We have found the Messiah' (that is, the Christ)."

PASTOR: Peter believed Jesus was the Son of God.

WOMEN: Jesus asked Peter, "'Who do you say I am?'

MEN: "Simon Peter answered, 'You are the Christ, the Son of the living God.'"

PASTOR: Jesus talked with a Samaritan woman beside the well at Sychar. She was amazed at what Jesus said. She hurried to call her friends so they could meet the prophet.

WOMEN: "Come, see a man who told me everything I ever did. Could this be the Christ?"

PASTOR: Mary and Martha grieved the death of their brother, Lazarus. In the midst of her sorrow, Martha testified of her faith in Jesus.

WOMEN: "'Yes, Lord,' she told [Jesus], 'I believe that you are the Christ, the Son of God.'"

PASTOR: Saul sought to imprison followers of Jesus. On the way to Damascus, however, he was bound by a blinding light. God changed Saul from a sightless detective to a living witness of the Messiah.

MEN: "Saul grew more and more powerful and baffled the Jews living in Damascus by proving that Jesus is the Christ."

PASTOR: We must make a decision about Jesus just as these biblical characters did. Is Jesus just a man who was a religious genius? Or is Jesus the Christ—the Anointed One—the Messiah?

CONGREGATION: "Everyone who believes that Jesus is the Christ is born of God."

PASTOR: Only those persons who invite Jesus to be Savior and Lord will live as a child of God.
    O come to my heart, Lord Jesus.

CONGREGATION: There is room in my heart for You.

Who's Got the Baby Jesus?

A Monologue

by Carroll Ferguson Hunt

(Woman enters, burdened with bags and packages, obviously holiday shopping. She can be any age, well-dressed, pleasant, sincere, a bit distracted. Big shoulder bag and long list in her hand. She moves to her assigned spot, drops her stuff, and checks over her list.)

Let's see . . . I've done all the kids *and* their teachers. The mail carrier, the newspaper kid. New cardigan for Mother. Fruitcake for Aunt Mabel. But I've got to mail it to Florida! Is there time? Oh, dear, I wonder . . .

(She begins talking to audience as if to a friend.) I don't see how I can squeeze in a trip to the post office on top of everything else, even for Aunt Mabel's fruitcake, do you? *(List again)* I have to bake cookies all day tomorrow. Can't do it then. We have an extra choir rehearsal this week for the Christmas music. The music this year's going to be simply *wonderful!* Can't miss that. Sally's angel costume is done, thank the Lord! *(Rolls eyes heavenward)* And You know I mean that, don't You?

But still I have our tree-trimming party to cook for—I always make my own egg nog—and Jack insists we go to his office party this year. I *must* find a new outfit for that. They really dress up. Here, I better write *that* down. *(Scribbles on list for a moment, then pauses and grows still)*

I get this way every year. I'm in a big fluster, aren't I? Seems like it happens every Christmas. Panic sets in and makes me miserable and, truth to tell, I make everyone around me miserable too. I get buried underneath my "good things to do" list, and so does everyone I know. Shopping and parties and cookies and new clothes, and . . . and . . . I find myself wondering why we're doing all this.

I'm not sure why, but it reminds me what happened in our Sunday School class last year. You remember? Sharon had this great idea, as she always does, that a different person take the figure of the Baby Jesus from the class crèche and keep it at home until next Sunday. We were supposed to center our week around Him, sort of, concentrate on Him . . . and we tried. We really did.

But about the third week when Jim and Sara took Him—or maybe it was Bonnie and her roommate—anyway, they lost Him! Couldn't find Him anywhere! They think it was during their present-wrapping blitz when they took one whole evening to do *all* their gift wrapping at once. Which isn't a bad idea, you know?

But, the point is, Baby Jesus disappeared! Gone!

The next Sunday when we all got to Sunday School we were dressed up in our holiday clothes—everyone looked terrific—and chewing away on the cinnamon buns Myrna brought to go with our coffee.

But there sat the poor little manger . . . empty! No Baby Jesus. Mary and Joseph and the shepherds all stood around peering at the straw with no reason that anyone could see. He wasn't there. We'd lost Him in all the hustle and con-fusion. And, I began to wonder if He would turn up at all, last Christmas. How do you admit to anyone that you've lost the Baby Jesus right out of the middle of Christmas?

I do hope we can keep track of Him this year.

(She wanders off, mumbling over her list and peering into her bags, not quite aware of what she has just said.)

The Critter Keeper

A Monologue
by Carroll Ferguson Hunt

(A man or overgrown boy enters. He is dressed in barnyard clothes, not cool jeans and T-shirt. Looks more slow than nerd-ish. If possible, an animal leans against him, maybe a cat on his shoulder. However, it must be silent and not distracting from the man's slow, hesitant speech, for it represents trust and illustrates his affinity with "critters.")

Um . . . I like critters. They like me, too, seems like. Why, ah, truth to tell, I like 'em better'n most people. *(Realizes that might be confusing)* Not better'n most people like critters, but better'n I like most people. 'Cause we-e-ll, people sometimes laugh at me . . . make fun, you know . . . but critters? Never. They just stand close and ask me to do stuff for 'em. I like that . . . an' I most generally know what they want and what to do about it.

Most folks 'round here ask me to see to their cows and donkeys and sheep . . . 'specially at birthin' time. I can usually help out. An' there's nothin' else I'd rather do . . . nothin' else I *can* do, far as that goes.

Few days back we had such a passel of folks here in town. Came to be counted and taxed, I heard tell. I didn't know so many folks called Bethlehem home. Filled up every inn and stoppin' place we got hereabouts.

Mighty strange feelin', so many people underfoot. Makes you feel all fluttery, like you wanta hide . . . which I was doin', kinda like . . . goin' along behind the houses and shops and inns, seein' to all the critters. Folks pay me to take care of 'em, so I did it real careful-like so they wouldn't be scared . . . like me . . . with all the extra people around.

I was real glad when I got to the cave behind the inn at the end of the street. Glad 'cause that's where I sleep, where I get away from folks. The innkeeper lets me stay up in the loft if I tend his milk goats and the donkeys that tote the firewood.

But . . . no gettin' away even in my cave, it turned out. That innkeeper went and rented out my cave to travelers . . . a man and his wife and their donkey! When I walked in and found 'em in my place . . . well, we just stood there and stared at each other, we were that surprised.

The innkeeper's goats did enough talkin' for the three of us, 'cause they always do. They came runnin' up to me and commenced to buttin' at my legs and chewin' on my clothes . . . kinda their way of sayin', "Glad to see you!"

Then the man's wife gave a terrible gasp and sank down into the straw . . . an' I saw she was in the family way . . . an' her baby had decided to come, never mind they didn't even have a proper room for the birthin'.

The man turned quick and knelt beside her . . . then he turned to me. We still didn't know what to say, so I nodded, gentle as I could, and penned them crazy goats off in the far corner. The donkeys had plenty of hay, I saw, so I asked 'em to lend me a bit. No problem there. I piled that there sweet-smellin', clean hay in a little manger . . . thought it might make a bed for the baby when the time came . . . then I looked at the man. He saw what I did and he nodded. He understood.

Now, you might think this peculiar, but I whispered to the goats and the donkeys that they should keep as still as can be, and that they should turn away and leave the man and his wife some peace. "Don't be starin' at 'em," said I to them. So they did what I said, like they always do. An' I climbed up into the loft.

Sure felt funny havin' someone else in my cave, but there wasn't anything I could do about that except wait 'til tax-payin' time in Bethlehem got over with.

We-e-ll, no need of my tellin' you about all the long time it took 'til that little lady's baby decided to come. I can tell you there was a whole lot of groanin' and whisperin' goin' on down in the stable. Then as time wore on, they quit whisperin' and just talked out loud, they was that worried. Didn't know nothin' about birthin', neither one of 'em. I could tell that right off. Then the man called up to me.

"Hello! Excuse me . . . could I ask you something?" Real polite-like, that he was. "Is there someone around to help my wife? She's . . . We . . . I can't . . ."

"I'm awful sorry, mister," I said. "This town is plumb crazy with so many extra people. Everyone's busy . . . an' the midwife died not two months ago."

It was then he started to cryin', poor man. First baby and no help. Had to be scary.

"I . . . uh, I done a lot of birthin' with critters hereabouts . . ." I could not believe my ears! Did I really say that? "I don't think they's a whole lot of a difference." I heard my mouth say. "I could stand way over there by the goats . . . you could tell me what's happenin' . . . an' I could tell you what to do." Boy, once this mouth got to workin', it wouldn't stop.

He said, "OK," and sounded real relieved. So, I climbed down . . . and we did it! We birthed that baby boy with no problem . . . an' as soon as the little fellow cried out for the first time on this earth, the goats and the donkeys sang out with him, like they was welcomin' him to the world.

And when the little mother wrapped her baby son in soft, clean cloths, she called me over. "Would you lay Him in the manger for me," she said. An' I did. I laid the little mite down on the clean hay, wonderin' all the while . . . what would all those people out there think if they only knew what happened in this stable tonight.

Do you reckon anyone ever heard such a tale before? an' don't you wonder what the little fellah grew up to be?

(He shrugs his shoulders and ambles off, muttering.) Sure would like to know whatever became of him. I suppose he might've . . .

Scrooge Plus
by Annette Dake

Cast: SCROOGE
GHOST

Setting: Christmastime at Scrooge's house—after the ghostly visits.

Props: Tinsel, pen and paper, plastic "Groucho" glasses and cigar

(At rise we see a happier SCROOGE *with tinsel around his neck. He is sitting at a desk writing a letter.)*

SCROOGE *(reading aloud as he writes):* Dear Timothy. So happy to hear from you again. Uncle Ebenezer loves you too. Concerning your proposal: not so sure financing a running shoe factory is such a great idea. What does "Reeboks" mean anyhow? I did especially like the crutch rental shop idea. Reasonable weekly rates. It has possibilities. We'll discuss it when you come home for Christmas. *(A knock at the door.* SCROOGE *answers it. No one is there. Continues writing. Pause. Another knock.)* Humbug! I mean, ho-hum, I wonder who it could be.

*(*GHOST *enters.)*

GHOST: Ebenezer Scrooge, I have come to warn you. If you do not change your ways, you are in danger of . . .

SCROOGE: Pardon me. You've made a serious error, or have incredibly bad timing!

GHOST: I am the Ghost of . . .

SCROOGE: Yes. Yes. Yes. You're a little late! I already played this scene with some friends of yours.

GHOST: Impostors!

SCROOGE: Impostors? They were great! Scared the meanness right out of me. I admit Christmas Past was sorta stuffy, but overall, a pretty transparent guy. *(Laughs robustly)* Transparent! Get it?

GHOST: Christmas Past is just that—past!

SCROOGE: But what about Christmas Present and Christmas Future? Christmas Future was too scary to not be real. Well, as real as you guys get anyway.

GHOST: Impostors all. I'm here to show you how to find true happiness.

SCROOGE: Look, like I told you, your buddies were already here. I hated people. People hated me. I mistreated Bob Cratchit. *(Under his breath)* He's still a scatter-brain. *(Cheering up)* But I'm learning to feel his pain! I'm Mr. Humanitarian!

GHOST: Are you happy in your heart?

SCROOGE: Define happy. I keep busy. I have friends. People love me, and I'm still rich! What's not to be happy?

GHOST: Let's talk futures market here.

SCROOGE: Already been there. Talk about scary. I realized if I didn't change, I'd die.

GHOST: News flash, Ebenezer! You're still going to die!

SCROOGE: That's just boo-tiful. Get it? *(Laughs)* Boo-tiful? Why do I always get the wise guys? I mean, die—as in alone, hated, despised.

GHOST: Things certainly have changed. No you're going to die alone, loved, and headed straight for hell.

SCROOGE: Wait just a penny-pinching minute! I'm a changed man. Nobody lives a better life than me. Ask anybody.

GHOST: That's why I'm here. Living a good life doesn't buy heaven when you die.

SCROOGE: Well, I'd like to know why not!

GHOST: Your good deeds are like filthy rags in God's eyes.

SCROOGE: Then why am I wasting my good time and hard-earned money on all this? What's the point? You ghosts are all alike. Promises, promises.

GHOST: You didn't do your research, Scrooge! A fine businessman like you listening to any Tom, Dick, or Airy that comes along! Airy! Get it?

SCROOGE: Why should I listen to you? I don't recall any formal introductions!

GHOST: I tried! I am the Ghost of God.

SCROOGE: Huh?

GHOST: The Holy Ghost, OK? I was just trying to stay in character with your story.

SCROOGE *(starts to leave):* I have some last-minute Christmas shopping to do for the Cratchit kids, so if you don't mind . . .

GHOST *(loudly):* Ebenezer Scrooge! Sit down! (SCROOGE *sits down.)* Remember when you asked the other night, "Is this all there is?" Well, we were listening. And I'm here to tell you, "No, this is not all there is."

SCROOGE: OK, you've got my attention! What else is there? I've got family, friends, fun, and fellowship.

GHOST: Peace of mind. Eternal life.

SCROOGE *(slowly):* OK, sign me up! Where do I buy it?

GHOST: It's already been bought.

SCROOGE: Is your sheet on too tight? Don't talk to me in riddles. How can I have eternal life?

GHOST *(pulls out cigar, Groucho glasses):* You just said the magic word! *(Takes off glasses)* There is One who already paid the price so you could have eternal life.

SCROOGE *(under his breath):* Sounds like something Bob Cratchitt would say. Humbug! I mean . . .

GHOST: His name is Jesus.

SCROOGE: Jesus? The Christmas Jesus? How did He buy eternal life?

GHOST: He was crucified—executed on a cross.

SCROOGE: Crucified? For what?

GHOST: For your sins, and the sins of humankind.

SCROOGE: For my sins?

GHOST: Is there an echo in here? Yes, for all those cruel, hateful things you and everyone else has done.

SCROOGE: Those other ghosts said I just had to change my ways, have an attitude adjustment . . .

GHOST: That's what the world wants you to believe. The truth is, we can't work our way into heaven. "For God so loved the world that he gave his one and only Son, that whoever believes in him shall not perish but have eternal life." Only God's Son, Jesus, can slam hell's door and open God's window. And, Scrooge . . . right now you make a better door than a window.

SCROOGE: Jesus loved me enough to die for me? Why? Because I cleaned up my life?

GHOST: Wrong. He loved you before you changed. He just wants you to love Him now and spend eternity in heaven with Him.

SCROOGE: How?

GHOST: Believe and ask Jesus to come into your heart.

SCROOGE: That's it?

GHOST: Not exactly. After Jesus comes into your life, you'll want to share His good news with others.

SCROOGE: Spirit, take me to see Jesus.

GHOST: Easier than that, Scrooge. You can ask Him to save you right here. It's called prayer.

SCROOGE: I can't believe I lost sleep over Past, Present, and Future when all the while I just needed Jesus. Thanks, Spirit!

GHOST: No, thank Jesus!

(GHOST *exits.* SCROOGE *bows his head in prayer, prays, then turns back to his letter.*)

SCROOGE: P.S. Timothy, when you get home, I have some good news to share with you. His name is Jesus. Love in Christ, Uncle Ebenezer.

(Curtain)

Real in Your Heart
by Chip Tutor

Cast: BEE
OSCAR
ELLIE
CHRISTMAS CAROLERS (offstage)

Setting: An office, decorated with efficient and slightly feminine taste. Office furnishings include a main desk and chair with an additional chair for visitors, a file cabinet with potted plant on top, portable tape player and headset, belt of "office supplies," hand vacuum, box, broom.

Props: Purse, stack of papers, wastebasket, coffee cup

(At rise: BEE *marches in angrily, slams her purse on the desk, and paces behind it, letting off steam. She wears a crisp business outfit and is obviously an efficient, goal-driven, professional woman, with no patience for the impractical or frivolous.)*

BEE: One sweater. One sweater left, and she had to have it. Of course she can have it . . . after her little brat wiped his snotty nose all over it. Who wants it? No telling how many viruses it's carrying now. *(She glances at her watch, then at the stack of paper piled neatly on her desk.)* The day's shot, and I have all this. *(She scoops up a handful and shuffles through it as she paces around. She creates a "priority" and a "later" pile on her desk; the "nots" she drops in the wastebasket.)* Priority . . . later . . . not . . . not . . . later . . . priority . . . priority . . . later . . . *(She collapses in her chair in resignation, singles out one sheet of paper, and begins working as she reassures herself calmly.)* One bite at a time. *(Deep breath and slowly)* One bite at a time.

(OSCAR, *a coworker and would-be suitor, enters with a cup of coffee and grins like a Chesire cat. His easy-come, easy-go attitude is almost as annoying as his harmless, yet persistent, amorous advances.* BEE *endures his relentless pursuit, which has become something of a game between them.)*

OSCAR: Hi, Bee. Busszzy?

(OSCAR *plops in the visitor chair without waiting for a reply, lounges casually, and swings one foot like a pendulum over the side while slurping his coffee.)*

BEE *(mostly ignoring him):* Oscar, has the world forgotten life exists beyond Christmas?

OSCAR: Bad day, huh?

(BEE *rises, begins stuffing papers in file folders, and thrusting them into the file cabinet.)*

31

BEE: I just blew the whole afternoon at the mall. One little item . . . that's all I wanted. Lunch was a stale corn dog while standing at an overcrowded counter. I had to eat with my elbows in puddles of ketchup and mustard so deep I practically needed a life preserver. *(She shows him the stains on her elbows to prove her point.)*

OSCAR: I'm trained in CPR. Need a little mouth . . .

BEE: Don't even say it. *(Pause, as if finally noticing him)* Oscar, is there a purpose to this visit, or are you just here to irritate me?

OSCAR: I'm obviously too late for that. But I do have good news—the workday is over. So let's clock out. Knock off. Blow this joint. Get down and outta here. Got any plans for dinner?

BEE: Paper work à la king. I thought Christmas was supposed to be a time of kindness and charity. So why do people act like animals? It took me all afternoon to find the sweater I was looking for, and then this *(searching for the appropriate word)* . . . rude lady practically elbowed me out of the way to get the last one before I did. I should have aced her out in the parking lot when I had the chance.

OSCAR: That would certainly be a most kind and charitable act.

BEE: Next I was run off the road by Ms. Suburban in her Jeep Cherokee who didn't see me cause the seat was piled to the roof with packages and her kids were wrestling in the back. Another holiday—exploited by retailers and greeting card companies.

OSCAR *(putting his cup on her desk)*: You forgot the "bah humbug."

BEE *(snatches the cup and pours it into the plant on top of the file cabinet)*: Spare me, Oscar, I don't have the time.

OSCAR: Hey, that was my coffee.

BEE: Regular, I hope. It hates decaf.

OSCAR: Listen . . . Bee . . . take your foot off the throttle . . . ease up . . . back off and enjoy the season.

BEE: Work does not stop because the world pauses for its token, once-a-year gesture of peace and goodwill.

OSCAR: No, but it does slow down a little . . . so take advantage of it . . . I do, and I'm an agnostic.

(BEE *slumps to her chair in resignation and resumes shuffling papers at a slower pace.)*

BEE: I guess you're right.

OSCAR: Of course I am . . . so relax. Loosen up. Take a break. It's Christmastime. Better than that, it's Friday. You going to the office party tonight?

BEE: I don't know. What I'd like to do is curl up on the sofa in front of a roaring fire and veg out. Instead, I have the office party tonight, shopping tomorrow, a Sunday School fellowship Saturday night, church with my mother on Sunday, then more shopping. How can I relax? And why are you so relaxed?

OSCAR: My shopping's done.

BEE: I thought men always waited till Christmas Eve.

OSCAR: Hey, I'm a '90s kind of guy. I shop through catalogs and QVC. I settle in on the couch with my remote, portable phone, chips, and beverage of my choice and let the gadgets do the walking. My only concern is developing a hangnail.

BEE: And high cholesterol.

OSCAR: OK. Go ahead and make fun, but my presents are pre-gift-wrapped and delivered UPS. And church has always been optional, so I don't have *that* millstone around my neck.

(OSCAR *puts his feet up on her desk, leans back, and smiles in self-satisfaction. Offstage,* CAROLERS *launch in to "Hark the Herald."* BEE *jumps out of her seat, shoves his feet off her desk, and stomps to the window.*)

BEE: Shut up!

(CAROLERS *abruptly stop.* BEE *returns to her desk and rearranges items in needless busyness.*)

OSCAR: Maybe if you gave up your religion, you wouldn't be so uptight.

BEE: I'm not giving up my religion—not totally anyway.

OSCAR: Then again, religion is good. Just keep it in its proper place—Christmas and Easter. That's what I do. (BEE *gives him a disapproving look.*) You never know, so why chance it? The rest of the year I worship in the comfort and convenience of home.

BEE: First Church of the Mattress and Springs?

OSCAR: I see you're familiar with my denomination. Ever been to a service?

BEE *(wryly):* Not as much as I'd like.

(OSCAR *gets up, takes her hands, and attempts to woo her with winsome charm.*)

OSCAR: What you need is soft music, candlelight, a quiet dinner. I know a nice little restaurant . . .

BEE: Oscar, not if I was a total atheist—and I'm close.

OSCAR: Well . . . I can see you want to work . . . alone. (He starts to leave.) But if you change your mind, I'll be down the street at T.G.I. Fridays.

BEE: Good-bye, Oscar.

OSCAR: OK, OK. I can take a hint. Why do I get the impression you don't want to go out with me?

(As OSCAR *leaves,* BEE *contemplates a moment, then opens her calendar.)*

BEE: Let's see, if I time it right . . . Hmmm . . . I wonder if I have any catalogs.

(As BEE *considers the possibilities,* ELLIE *bursts through the door singing Amy Grant's "Sing Your Praise to the Lord" at the top of her lungs. She is the clean-up girl at the office. She is a hybrid collection of gregarious, childlike exuberance, oddball individuality bordering on eccentricity, unsophisticated transparency, and candid homespun philosophy. She wears faded cotton sweats, old tennis shoes, a headband, and a headset. A western holster belts her waist, dangling numerous janitorial objects such as garbage bags, rags, a feather duster, and a hand vacuum. She carries a cardboard file box, which is also full of supplies and a broom clamped under her arm. She sets the box on the floor and alternates using her broom as a guitar and microphone as she bounces around, performing for an unseen audience.*

ELLIE *(finishing her song):* Sing! Sing! Sing! Whoa! *(She stops startled when she notices* BEE *watching in amusement. Instinctively,* ELLIE *draws the hand vac from her holster and aims it defensively.* BEE *"gasps" and* ELLIE *stops, looks at the vac, then smiles sheepishly.)* Don't worry. It's not loaded.

BEE: Are you?

ELLIE *(smiles knowingly):* Quite a get-up, huh? But it works for me. *(She blows imaginary smoke from the barrel of the hand vac and holsters it.)* Best sucker-upper east [west] of the Mississippi.

BEE *(in disbelief):* You're the cleaning lady?

ELLIE *(salutes):* Ellie Sue Sanderson and Immaculate Office Incorporated. Hey, if I knew I was the floor show, I'd have worn an evening gown.

BEE: I didn't mean it like that, it's just that . . .

ELLIE: I know. I'm atypical. A square peg. A rare bird. But, I grow on you. Kinda like a fungus. My favorite professor calls me a cartoon.

BEE: A cartoon?

ELLIE: Yeah, you know . . . loony tunes? But what does he know. Those psych profs don't have much to talk about, know what I mean?

BEE: You're in college?

ELLIE *(proudly):* Seventh year senior psychology major. You didn't think I was planning to do this all my life, did you?

BEE: Well, I . . .

ELLIE: But don't worry, I'm not one of those who goes around analyzing every-body, OK? Although, I hope you don't mind my saying you look really stressed. *(She pops a wad of bubble gum in her mouth and chomps on it with loud smacking and popping. Then she sits on the file box and crosses her legs in a listening pose.)* So talk.

BEE *(trying to give a hint):* Talking isn't the problem, it's all the work I can't get done.

ELLIE *(props elbow under chin):* Uh-huh.

BEE *(harder):* Because of so many interruptions?

ELLIE *(after a pause, then jumps to her feet):* Hey, I get the message. You don't have to hit me on the side of the head with a two by four. *(Thinking)* Though Mom says that's probably the best way to get my attention. *(Knocks her head emphatically with the heel of her hand)* Like a rock. You go right ahead and work. I'll be quiet as a churchmouse.

(ELLIE *picks up the broom and starts sweeping as* BEE *returns to her paper-work. As* ELLIE *sweeps, she pauses to add more sticks of gum, forming a huge wad that she cracks and pops in an irritating manner. Distracted,* BEE *rises and returns to filing. As* BEE *leaves her seat,* ELLIE *begins dusting around the desk, forcing* BEE *to wait, impatiently, for* ELLIE *to finish so she can sit down.* BEE *fi-nally speeds up the process by picking up items so* ELLIE *can dust underneath.)*

BEE: I don't want to begrudge people their right to enjoy the holidays, but isn't all the sentiment a bit overworked?

ELLIE: You mean Christmas? It's more than sentiment. Christmas is a spiritual season. A time when people search for life's deeper meanings. Some even find it.

BEE: Like explaining to your credit card company you didn't "mean" to get so "deep" in dept.

(ELLIE *stops to philosophize, punctuating the air with her rag, as she crescen-dos dramatically.)*

ELLIE: OK, so it is a bit commercialized. Still, there's an atmosphere of antici-pation, of excitement. You see it in eager faces. Hear it in joyful music. Smell and taste it in the crisp night air. You can almost reach out and grasp it. Something spectacular is about to happen. Like that first Christmas long ago. It's like an electrical charge. Can't you feel it?

BEE: Sure, it zaps me right in the pocketbook. Hasn't anybody ever told you Christmas is for kids?

ELLIE: Yeah, I'm a kid at heart. But, hey, the Word says you have to accept the kingdom of God like a child; and be honest, isn't there something about Christmas that's different, that's special? I mean, you can't put it into words, but you know it's there, inside.

BEE: I don't know, maybe I used to care, when I was a little girl. I remember I couldn't sleep a wink Christmas Eve. I kept sneaking downstairs to peek at all the presents under the tree.

ELLIE: See? And I bet those warm emotions are still there, just waiting to break free. Go with that, let it out.

BEE: I've learned not to let nostalgic mush affect my sensibilities.

ELLIE: Maybe we should.

BEE: I don't think so. Christmas is only a drain, and when it's over, my time, energy, and finances are all spent. My goal is simply to survive it and get on with life, hopefully with enough in the bank to pay January's bills.

ELLIE: Survival I can relate to. That's how it was after Dad's funeral, but we managed. Love can pull you through the darkest times.

BEE: Just like the Waltons, huh?

ELLIE: Who?

BEE: Never mind.

ELLIE *(tosses BEE a box):* Here, make yourself useful.

BEE: What's this?

ELLIE: Plant food. My first month here, it almost died. But with a little extra care, it perked right up.

BEE: I thought it was because of my encouraging talks to it.

ELLIE: Then the poor thing was probably dying from depression.

BEE: What do you mean?

ELLIE: No offense, but you've got a bad case of the me, myself, and I's. *(She douses the plant with water from a plastic water bottle; squirts some in her mouth, then swipes her sleeve across her mouth.)* Ah, spring water. Can't beat it.

BEE *(pouring food on the plant):* Maybe I am making a big case out of it.

ELLIE: A federal one.

BEE: OK. But, admit it, there's all this hype—a big build-up—then it's over and nothing—just an aching emptiness. It makes the whole thing seem so unreal.

ELLIE: First, it has to be real in your heart.

BEE: How does that happen? A sprinkle of fairy dust?

ELLIE: By giving. *(She blows a mammoth bubble that explodes on her face.)* Boy, that was a big one.

BEE *(picks up the plant and caresses it fondly):* You're starting to sound like the preacher at my mother's church.

ELLIE: Me? A preacher? Go figure, huh?

BEE: That's why I go as little as possible—which would be less if Mother didn't still drag me along. *(Mimics pastor)* God loves a cheerful giver. Then they pass the offering plate with this holy smile.

ELLIE: Maybe you haven't given the right gift.

BEE: I've never known anyone to refuse money.

ELLIE: Refuse, no. But God wants more than that. And it's a good thing, too, because I, like, give the widow's mite.

BEE: God wants something other than money? I must have been in the wrong church.

(ELLIE *whips a plastic bag off her belt and snaps it open to empty the waste can. She struggles to hold the bag open and get the can inside, so* BEE, *who is growing annoyed, puts the plant down, grabs the can, and empties it into the bag that* ELLIE *holds open with two hands.)*

ELLIE: Every year I take Christmas baskets to nursing homes. In fact, I'm going tonight when I finish here.

BEE: What's so special about that?

(ELLIE *ties up the garbage bag, collects her equipment, and loads her tray.)*

ELLIE *(shrugs):* When you see those faces light up, you know you've made a difference. It's, like, internally and eternally cool.

BEE *(cynically):* I know. "It's more blessed to give than to receive."

ELLIE: The Lord's words. I know because in my Bible it's in red ink. He set the example, so it must be high on His "to do" list.

(BEE *goes back behind her desk and shuffles more papers into piles while* ELLIE *takes the dust vac and cleans around the top of the walls, then along her sweat pants.)*

ELLIE: Man, those little fuzz balls are such a pain.

BEE: Yes, the example. Jesus, the great teacher, a man of loving compassion, selfless giving, and spiritual insight.

ELLIE: Preach it, sister!

BEE: Of course, they killed Him.

ELLIE: Of course, that was part of the plan. You see, He wasn't just a man or a great teacher; He was the Lord. He didn't stay dead; He rose again and lives today in people. People make Jesus real. And when you make Him real for others, He becomes real to you.

BEE: Yeah, well, I quit believing fairy tales a long time ago.

ELLIE: Can you give me a hand with this desk?

(Both scoot the desk aside and ELLIE *cleans underneath while* BEE *is forced again to wait and watch. She moves both chairs impatiently so* ELLIE *can get underneath.)*

BEE: Do you always enlist other people to help with your work?

ELLIE: Are you kidding? No one is ever around when I work. But you've forgotten about yourself, haven't you?

BEE: You set me up.

ELLIE: Yeah, I know, but it worked, didn't it? When you're busy helping others, you forget about yourself.

BEE: Thanks for the object lesson. Now may I get back to my work?

ELLIE: Sure thing. I'll just move along. *(She draws the hand vac and waves it around.)* Look out, cobwebs, I'm armed and disinfected. Oh, by the way, I came across this file box while I was cleaning a closet. It looked personal, so I didn't want to throw anything away. If you need me, I'll be in Mr. Bradley's office. It has a great view of the city, with all the Christmas lights on. It's totally awesome.

(ELLIE *turns and hands the box to* BEE, *who gives it a cursory glance.)*

BEE: It looks like old papers of mine. I can't imagine how it got here. Well, just leave it. I'll go through it and make sure there's nothing here I want to keep.

(ELLIE *holsters the vac, hooks her thumbs in the belt, assumes a bowlegged cowboy stance, and impersonates John Wayne.)*

ELLIE: Well, I want to tell ya, pilgrim, I'm gonna get on my prize horsey and ride on out of here. *(She tips the imaginary Stetson and swaggers off as* BEE *starts looking through the file box. She picks out a paper and reads aloud.)*

BEE: This certifies that Beatrice Anderson is the fourth grade spelling champion. I didn't get the name "Spelling Bee" Anderson for nothing. Hmmm. 1978 high school yearbook editor. Eighth grade student class president. The first female class president in Centerville history. Bible drill participant. Now that really goes back. *(Pulls out a letter)* What's this?

Dear Santa,

    I am seven years old and would like the following: a Barbie doll, a new dress, a front row ticket to the Beatles concert. *(Interrupts her reading)* What I saw in Ringo, I'll never know. *(Continues)* Also, Santa, please make Mommy happy. She has been sad ever since Daddy left. She works hard and acts brave, but I know she's pretending. She said we might not get all the presents we want this year since things are a little tight. But I know you can bring all the presents we need. My friend Margaret says she doesn't believe in Santa Claus cause she saw her parents putting presents under the tree. But I don't listen to Margaret. She's kinda dumb. I know you're busy, Santa, and there are lots of other kids too. So if I can have only one present, then please make my mommy happy. She doesn't smile like she used to, and I really miss seeing her smile. I would give all my other presents just for that. I know you can do it, Santa. I believe in you. Sincerely, Bee.

It took a lot of years for that letter finally to be answered. I guess I stopped believing in Santa Claus years before Mom ever smiled again. Maybe when I lost my faith in Santa, I lost my faith in the Lord. I suppose I believed in my head, but not really in my heart.

God, I'm sorry for making Christmas just an event and forgetting the faith that makes it so real. Be real again, Lord, so I might make You real to someone else.

(ELLIE *returns and interrupts the prayer.*)

ELLIE: Oh, sorry. I just wanted to let you know I was taking off.

BEE: It's all right. Say, would you like a hand with those baskets?

ELLIE: You know me. I never refuse a little help.

BEE: Good. Let's go.

ELLIE: I thought there was an office party tonight.

BEE: You're right. Should we invite them along?

ELLIE: You know, I think I could get to like you.

BEE: Thanks. I'm beginning to think that myself. (BEE *throws her coat on, and they start out the door as* OSCAR *enters.*) C'mon, Oscar, you're coming with us.

OSCAR: Where are we going?

BEE: To deliver Christmas baskets.

OSCAR: Fine with me. So, Bee, is this a date?

BEE: Not on your life. But if you're nice, I'll let you open the door for me.

OSCAR *(shrugs):* It's a start. I can live with that.

(They all exit together. Curtain.)

The Littlest Star
by Enelle Eder

Cast: NARRATOR
STAR ONE
STAR TWO
STAR THREE
LITTLE STAR
STAR MASTER
STAR CHOIR

Setting: The heavens

Props: Papers, clipboard

(NARRATOR *speaks in the darkness.*)

NARRATOR: "In the beginning God created the heaven and the earth. And the earth was without form, and void; and darkness was upon the face of the deep. And the spirit of God moved upon the face of the waters. And God said, Let there be light: and there was light. And God saw the light, that it was good: and God divided the light from the darkness. And God called the light Day, and the darkness he called Night. And the evening and the morning were the first day.

"And God said, Let there be a firmament in the midst of the waters, and let it divide the waters from the waters. And God made the firmament, and divided the waters which were under the firmament from the waters which were above the firmament: and it was so. And God called the firmament Heaven. And the evening and the morning were the second day.

"And God said, Let the waters under the heaven be gathered together unto one place, and let the dry land appear: and it was so. And God called the dry land Earth; and the gathering together of the waters called he Seas: and God saw that it was good. And God said, Let the earth bring forth grass, the herb yielding seed, and the fruit tree yielding fruit after his kind, whose seed is in itself, upon the earth: and it was so. And the earth brought forth grass, and herb yielding seed after his kind, and the tree yielding fruit, whose seed was in itself, after his kind: and God saw that it was good. And the evening and the morning were the third day.

"And God said, Let their be lights in the firmament of the heaven to divide the day from the night: and let them be for signs, and for seasons, and for days, and years: and let them be for lights in the firmament of the heaven to give light upon the earth: and it was so. And God made two great lights, the greater light to rule the day, and the lesser light to rule the night:

"He made the stars also . . ." [KJV].

(*Light up as the* STARS *enter, laughing and playing.*)

STAR ONE: I can hardly wait until my name is called. I will have my own special spot in the sky, and I bet I can shine brighter than any star ever placed.

STAR TWO: You're such a show-off. I'm just glad to have been selected at all.

STAR THREE: That's right. We could be like that scrawny little star over there. I hear she was told to wait for another time before she gets her position in the sky.

STAR ONE: Well, I can believe that. She certainly isn't as big as we are.

STAR TWO: Uh-oh! Shape up, you guys, here comes the Star Master.

(Everyone hurries to get in line. STAR MASTER enters.)

STAR MASTER: All right, you little twinks! I'm here to give you your orders, so listen up! Once you have a spot it will be your responsibility to be there every day at dusk and remain there until sunrise in the morning. There will be no sleeping on this job, and you will keep yourself shined up and in tip-top shape! Is that clear?

STARS: Yes Sir!

STAR MASTER: I can't hear you!

STARS *(loudly):* Yes Sir!

STAR MASTER: OK. Now, here are your papers with directions. So follow them carefully, and you won't get into each other's light.

(STAR MASTER *hands out papers to all the stars except* LITTLE STAR, *who is waiting at the end of the line. All the other stars read their papers and talk to themselves or friends. All slowly exit, except for* STAR MASTER *and* LITTLE STAR.)

LITTLE STAR *(quietly approaching* STAR MASTER): Excuse me, Sir.

STAR MASTER: Huh, who said that?

LITTLE STAR: Excuse me, I'm down here. *(Waves her arms)*

STAR MASTER: Oh, there you are. What seems to be your problem?

LITTLE STAR: Well, you did not give me an assigned spot.

STAR MASTER: Let me check my papers here. *(Flips through the papers on his clipboard)* Ah, yes, here it is, the boss has decided that you need to grow some more before he can place you. So, you'll just have to wait. Sorry, kid.

(LITTLE STAR *turns away, dejected.* STAR MASTER *turns back to his papers and exits.)*

(Optional musical interlude with STAR CHOIR)

NARRATOR: Many years went by until one day all the stars were called together.

(STARS *and* STAR MASTER *enter, talking excitedly, wondering what the commotion is all about.)*

STAR MASTER: OK. Let's have it quiet in here! I have a very important assignment for you. The boss has decided that he needs a million stars to form a pillar of fire to lead the children of Israel. *(Excited reaction from* STARS*)* Now, we have most of the stars chosen, but I have called you together because we need a few more. Some of you are going to be fortunate enough to help with this assignment. *(Starts down the row)* Now, let me see, I'll take you and you and you, and oh yes, you there. *(He chooses all but* LITTLE STAR.*)*

(LITTLE STAR *waves excitedly in the background.)*

LITTLE STAR: Oh, excuse me.

STAR MASTER: What? Oh, you again.

LITTLE STAR: Yes, Sir. You forgot to pick me.

STAR MASTER: Huh? No, I didn't forget about you. The boss said that you still need to do some growing. But look, kid, I'm sure that someday the boss will have a special job just for you. *(He turns around and starts to exit; laughs to himself.)* Yeah, right.

LITTLE STAR *(determined):* I'll show them! I am going to find my own spot. *(Exits)*

NARRATOR: And the little star did try. Sometimes she would sneak behind a cloud and pop out at night to light the way for some weary traveler, but God would always call her back and tell her to be patient because someday her chance would come.

The centuries were rolling by, and the little star was getting bigger and brighter every day. Then finally, her chance came.

(STARS *enter, excitedly chatting again, wondering what is happening.* LITTLE STAR *comes in last.)*

STAR MASTER: There you are. Get over here. It's time. Hurry up!

LITTLE STAR *(running over):* What's all the excitement about, Sir?

STAR MASTER: It's time! It's time! You get to do the special job. I always knew you would get your break, kid! Now, here's the location. Get up there and shine like you've never shone before!

LITTLE STAR: Yes, Sir! I will do my best!

(The lights dim as all other STARS *exit.* LITTLE STAR *moves to the front and center. The only light is a spotlight right on her. She holds her hands out, "shining.")*

NARRATOR: And did that little star ever shine! She twinkled all over with excitement and shone like no other star ever had before. She looked down and saw wise men moving toward her. She saw shepherds in their fields. And she saw angels singing of Messiah's birth.

Then she knew. It was time. And she shone brighter still as she realized that her light was showing the way to the greatest Light of all.

Lights in the Darkness
by James C. Tillman

Cast: NEHEMIAH: *head angel*
SETH: *angel*
ELEAZAR: *angel*
SHIMANI: *angel*
ZADOK: *angel*
FATANA: *angel*
TEACHER
MARCELLOUS
BANIE
BARUK
JANET
LYNNE
EXTRAS

Setting: Scene 1: The main offices of "Angel Publicity, Inc."

Scene 2: A first-century classroom

Scene 3: A modern living room with piano

Props: Checkers set, dart set, charts and graphs, several large old books, cup

Scene 1

(At rise, a number of angels are hanging out at what appears to be an office. A large sign is on the wall: "Angel Publicity: Ideas That Fly." SETH, ELEAZAR, SHIMANI, ZADOK, and FATANA are lounging about. ELEAZAR is napping, ZADOK and FATANA are playing darts, and SETH and SHIMANI are playing checkers.)

SHIMANI *(after making six jumps):* King me.

SETH: Hey! You moved when I wasn't looking.

SHIMANI: Who me?

SETH: Yes, you, Beelzebub breath.

SHIMANI: What are you talking about? I jumped you fair and square.

SETH: You wouldn't know fair and square if it rose up and bit you on your . . .

ZADOK *(lining up a dart toss):* Would you guys keep it down, you're ruining my concentration.

SETH: Well, that's it. I'm not playing with a cheater.

SHIMANI: You're just sore because I always win.

SETH: You don't always win.

FATANA: Face it, Seth, you haven't won since the Garden of Eden Tournament.

SETH: Why are you guys always picking on me?

ZADOK: We're not always picking on you, Seth.

SETH: Yes, you are. You always call me dumb and stupid.

SHIMANI: Hey, we're angels. We can't lie.

ZADOK *(sarcastic):* Come on, fellahs, we're being a little hard on old Seth, aren't we? After all, he came up with some of our best ideas.

SETH: Yeah.

ZADOK: Like when Moses needed some help finding his way in the desert, what was your idea again?

SETH *(mumbling):* A pillar of ice.

ZADOK: What was that?

SETH: A pillar of ice.

ZADOK: Great idea! It's hot in the desert, right? They'll need some ice, right? Too bad your pillar of ice became a puddle of mud. It was a good thing Nehemiah caught it before the boss found out.

SHIMANI: Hey, remember his idea for the rainbow?

FATANA: Oh, that was a great one. Instead of brilliant colors after a cleansing rain, you wanted the clouds to spell out, "Yea, God!"

SETH: Well, you've got to admit, it would have gotten their attention.

FATANA: It was a good thing Nehemiah came up with the rainbow idea. *(Looking around)* Hey, where is Nehemiah anyway?

SHIMANI: He said he had to go upstairs for a management meeting. Something big is up, I can tell.

ZADOK: Oh, not another seven plagues. Remember how hard it was to come up with those seven original plagues?

SHIMANI: According to Nehemiah, its even bigger than that.

SETH: Maybe it will be big enough to wake up Eleazar.

FATANA: He's been sleeping right there for, what *(looks at watch)*, going on a hundred years? Do you think we should wake him up?

(ELEAZAR *lets loose with a big snore.*)

ALL *(after looking over at* ELEAZAR *then back at each other):* Naaaah.

(NEHEMIAH *breezes in with a businesslike air.*)

NEHEMIAH: OK. I want everyone over here. We've got a project, and this one needs everything we've got!

SHIMANI: Should I wake Eleazar?

NEHEMIAH: Nah, let him sleep. We'll wake him if we need him.

SHIMANI: So what's the project?

NEHEMIAH: As you know, whenever the boss gets an idea, he gives us the task of making it work. Up to now, his ideas have been things like how to get Moses' attention.

SETH: The burning bush.

NEHEMIAH: Yeah, like the burning bush. Up till now these jobs have been pretty ordinary. But now, whoa, well . . . you guys just aren't going to believe this one. *(Pause)* The boss wants to go to earth.

(Silence)

SHIMANI *(dumbfounded):* Why? What would make him want to do that? Talk about your lousy vacation spots.

NEHEMIAH: He doesn't want to visit. He wants to live there.

ZADOK *(in disgust):* Live there!

FATANA: Hey, that might not be so bad. He could look at it as a fixer-upper. A little rearrangement of the landscape. Wipe out a nation or two, and hey, it might be livable.

NEHEMIAH: You guys don't get it. He doesn't want to change a thing. He wants to go there just as it is.

(Same silence)

SHIMANI: Come on. You gotta be kidding.

FATANA: Well, OK. Let's think this through. He could take over a kingdom somewhere and rule from a well-appointed palace *(taking the role of an interior decorator).* We could do the throne room in purple . . . no, lavender. And the wallpaper, oh, what we could do with wallpaper . . . ?

(ALL *chime in with their ideas about the decorations.)*

NEHEMIAH *(whistles for silence):* Quiet! *(Silence)* Now, let me tell you the whole story.

SETH: There's more?

NEHEMIAH: Oh yeah. He doesn't want to live in a palace or rule a kingdom or have a lavender throne room. (FATANA *looks hurt.)* What he wants to do is be born a human to a poor Jewish carpenter in a small suburb of Jerusalem.

(Silence)

SETH *(sarcastic):* Is that all?

NEHEMIAH: As a matter of fact, no. He doesn't want to be born in a house. He wants to be born in a stable.

SETH: Why, Nehemiah? Why does he want to degrade himself like that?

NEHEMIAH: Only one reason I can think of. He loves them. *(Pause, then matter-of-factly)* So, OK, let's get on with our part of the plan.

ZADOK: And that is?

NEHEMIAH: We're supposed to come up with a sign that announces his birth.

ZADOK: A sign? You mean he wants people to know about this?

NEHEMIAH: Not everyone.

SHIMANI: Let me guess. Just lowlifes and degenerates.

NEHEMIAH: Well, yes and no. He wants a certain group of royalty and a bunch of shepherds to know about his birth.

FATANA: Oh fine! We have to let both ends of the social spectrum know about the same birth at the same time!

NEHEMIAH: You got it. Now think!

(ALL *begin to pace and go through exaggerated motions of brainstorming.*)

SHIMANI: I got it. We could advertise in the *Jerusalem Times* under royalty and shepherds.

NEHEMIAH: No good. Shepherds don't read much.

(Back to brainstorming)

ZADOK: Hey, how about another hand writing on the wall. It worked pretty good for Belshazzar.

FATANA: No walls in a pasture.

NEHEMIAH: It's got to be something simple, yet profound. Something that can't be missed.

(Brainstorming)

SETH *(quietly):* How about a star?

NEHEMIAH: What did you say?

SETH: A star.

SHIMANI *(sarcastic):* Yeah, right! A star. What's that you're using for brains?

SETH: No, listen. We could put a star, a new star, right over the stable.

NEHEMIAH *(before* SHIMANI *can make another comment):* Hey! That's a great idea. A star, the shepherds can see a star, and the royal folks can see it too. I think it might just work. What do the rest of you think?

(Pause to look at each other, then back at NEHEMIAH. *All give their agreement.)*

ZADOK: Hey, what about Eleazar? Should we get his opinion?

NEHEMIAH: I suppose so. Yeah. Wake him up. Let's see what he thinks.

(All huddle around ELEAZAR *as* SHIMANI *and* NEHEMIAH *jar him awake.)*

ELEAZAR *(drowsily):* What's going on?

NEHEMIAH: Now listen up. The boss wants to go to earth, see, but he doesn't want to go as a king. He wants to be born in a stable, the son of a carpenter. It's our job to come up with a way to tell a bunch of shepherds and a few kings where he will be born. Seth thinks a star over the stable will work. What do you think?

ELEAZAR *(yawns and sits up to look around):* Sounds fine, guys . . . *(stretches and yawns),* but will they even look up to see a star?

(ELEAZAR *looks up and they all follow his gaze, then freeze as blackout.)*

Scene 2

(At rise. MARCELLOUS *is sitting at the back desk, staring off into the sky.* BANIE *and* BARUK *are paying attention to* TEACHER. *They are all dressed to give the impression of a classroom in the Far East during the first century. This is an astronomy class, and graphs and charts are scattered throughout the room.* TEACHER *is checking homework.)*

TEACHER: Very good, Prince Baruk. You are coming along quite nicely with your equations. And you, Prince Banie, you seem to have understood the latest question. And you, Prince Marcellous *(looking at* MARCELLOUS' *paper)* have succeeded in producing nothing in the last hour! Why do you try my patience so? What have you been doing with your time? (MARCELLOUS *begins to speak.)* No! Don't tell me. You have been gazing at the stars.

MARCELLOUS: After all, our father the king has hired you to teach us about the stars, not nonsense from dusty old books!

TEACHER: Is that what you think of my teaching? Is all that I have taught you nonsense? Just nonsense?

BANIE: We do seem to spend a lot of time with your books.

TEACHER: And for good reason! You cannot understand the stars until you understand my books!

BARUK: What do you mean, Teacher? We don't understand how these books are going to tell us about the stars.

TEACHER *(begging heaven):* Give me patience! All right, everyone, look up. *(Puzzled looks from students)* Look up, I say! *(They all look up.)* What do you see?

BANIE: The sky?

TEACHER: How observant. And what is in the sky?

MARCELLOUS: Stars.

TEACHER *(dryly):* You do have a profound mind, Marcellous. Now, what do the stars mean?

BARUK: Mean?

TEACHER: Yes. What is their purpose? Why do they exist?

BANIE: Well, I have heard it said in the marketplace that they are the thousand eyes of a thousand-headed black serpent. When they twinkle, he is winking at us.

TEACHER: How imaginative if not scientific. And you, Prince Marcellous, why do you think they exist?

MARCELLOUS: For some reason, I believe they were created to tell us something about God.

TEACHER: And what are they telling us?

MARCELLOUS: I just don't know. Or, maybe I'm not smart enough to understand.

TEACHER: Or maybe you're looking in the wrong place.

MARCELLOUS: Wrong place?

TEACHER: Prince Baruk, would you please go over to that shelf and bring me one of my dusty old books? (BARUK *does so and brings back a large book.*) Yes, that is the one. Now, turn to the 19th chapter and begin reading.

BARUK *(after finding the reference):* "The heavens declare the glory of God; the skies proclaim the work of his hands. Day after day they pour forth speech; night after night they display knowledge."

TEACHER: Thank you. That is enough. What does that tell us?

BANIE: That the stars are there to tell us about God.

TEACHER: Exactly! Now, normally they just tell us general things about His power and creativity and that sort of thing. But *(dramatic pause)* lately, He has told us something very specific. He has told us where He will be born.

MARCELLOUS: God will be born?

TEACHER: Is there an echo in here? Of course, He will be born. In another of my "dusty old books" is written: "For to us a child is born, to us a son is given, and the government will be on his shoulders. And he will be called Wonderful Counselor, Mighty God, Everlasting Father, Prince of Peace."

BARUK: But how do you know where He will be born?

BANIE: Or when?

TEACHER: Where is told us, "But you, Bethlehem, in the land of Judah, are by no means least among the rulers of Judah; for out of you will come a ruler who will be the shepherd of my people Israel." And the when is something I have waited a long, long time for. But now the time has come.

MARCELLOUS: The time has come for what, Teacher? How do you know the time has come?

TEACHER: Prince Marcellous, if you had spent more time studying the stars instead of just gazing at them, you would have seen it.

ALL: Seen what?

TEACHER: Seen that. *(He points to a place above the audience. The students all follow his finger and stare transfixed. While the students stare,* TEACHER *goes over to a chart.)* And unless my calculations are off, it is directly over . . . Bethlehem.

BANIE: Did you ever see such a beautiful star?

BARUK: How long has it been there?

MARCELLOUS: How could we have missed it?

TEACHER: Take heart, Prince Marcellous, you and a few million other people have missed it.

MARCELLOUS: But can't they see it? Don't they understand what it means?

TEACHER: Yes, they can see it. But, no, they don't understand what it means without this *(holds up Bible).* It is just an exceptionally beautiful star among a host of beautiful stars.

BARUK: We are going, aren't we? To see God born?

TEACHER: Of course you are going.

BANIE: But you're coming, too, aren't you, Teacher?

BARUK: We need you to guide us.

TEACHER: No. I am too old. The journey would be my end. But you will find the way. Just follow the star. The star will be your guide to the King.

MARCELLOUS: But are we the only ones going? What about all the other princes in other kingdoms?

TEACHER: Somehow it seems right to send just you three.

BARUK: But what should we give as gifts? We must bring gifts!

BANIE: How about a thousand sheep?

MARCELLOUS: We can't very well go tramping through the desert with a thousand sheep. No, it's got to be small but valuable.

TEACHER: I'm sure you'll come up with something fit for a king.

MARCELLOUS: Teacher, what do we do when we get there?

TEACHER: So many questions! The one who gave you these words *(the Bible)* and a star to guide you will guide your hearts as you worship the Child. Now be off with you. I have a few more dusty old books to read before I sleep tonight. *(The students exit.* TEACHER *goes over to another shelf, takes down a book and begins to read.)* "The people living in darkness have seen a great light; on those living in the land of the shadow of death a light has dawned."

(Fade to blackout.)

Scene 3

(At rise, a group of EXTRAS *stand around a piano. They are quietly talking and singing Christmas carols.* LYNNE *drifts off from the group. As the music continues to play, she moves to center stage.* JANET *notices her missing and moves away to look for her.)*

ALL: O, Star of wonder, star of night. Star with royal beauty bright. Westward leading, still proceeding, guide us to thy perfect light . . .

JANET: There you are. What are you doing out here? It's cold.

LYNNE: Just looking.

JANET: You couldn't pick a better night for stargazing. It must be 20 degrees *[or other appropriate temperature]*. I brought you some hot apple cider *(hands her the cider)*.

LYNNE: Thanks.

(Pause)

JANET: You seem to be in a pensive mood tonight. Are you all right?

LYNNE: I guess so. *(She looks back up at the stars.)*

JANET: Quite the conversationalist too. So, see any new constellations? *(Pause, then announcer's voice)* Ladies and gentlemen, I would like to direct your attention to the newest discovery in astronomical science. It is the Oreo Constellation. Named thus due to its large cluster of stars with a black hole on either side. *(No reaction from* LYNNE*)* Hey, if you're not going to laugh at my jokes, I'm going inside.

LYNNE: I'm sorry Janet, were you talking to me?

JANET: No, Santa Claus just stopped by for directions.

LYNNE: That's nice.

JANET: OK, that's it. I don't know what you see so enchanting about standing out on the patio in this frigid weather, but I'm going in before I die of exposure! *(She starts to leave.)*

LYNNE: Have you ever wondered what it was like?

JANET: OK, I'll bite. What what was like?

LYNNE: The star over Bethlehem.

JANET: Well, I guess it was . . . bright.

LYNNE: Then why didn't everyone go to see Jesus? Why only a few?

JANET: Good question. You should ask the pastor.

LYNNE: Tonight when he was speaking about people being blind to the light, it really got me thinking.

JANET: Is this going to be one of your deep discussions? Because if it is, could we please find someplace where I can feel the tip of my nose?

LYNNE *(ignoring):* I was thinking about all those people living, working, and playing under that star. They never even knew it could lead them to the most wonderful event the world had ever seen.

JANET *(giving in to the conversation):* I guess they were too busy.

LYNNE: That's exactly what I thought too.

JANET: Good. Then we both agree. Let's go in before I lose the use of both legs. *(Stretches legs and begins to exit)*

JANET: But then I thought, how can you be too busy to miss a star? All you have to do is look up!

JANET: I don't mean to be simplistic, but maybe they didn't look up.

LYNNE: Do we look up?

JANET: One of us does, that's for certain.

LYNNE: No, Janet, I really mean this. When do you and I look up for the star?

JANET: I have followed you so far, but now you aren't making sense. The star is gone. It disappeared thousands of years ago.

LYNNE: I don't think so. I think the star is still out there.

JANET: Where?

LYNNE: We find it whenever we look up, whenever anyone looks for the true light, God sends them a star.

JANET: You're not talking about the sky anymore, are you?

LYNNE: Remember that time when it was really tough with Tom and me?

JANET: Yeah. That was a struggle.

LYNNE: It was as if I were in a black hole. Everything around me was dark. I was scared, and I prayed, more than I ever prayed in my life. I can't even remember what I prayed for, exactly, but what I think I really wanted was light. And God gave me a star.

JANET: What was that?

LYNNE: You. You were that star. God shone through you every time we talked. You read Scripture with me, and we prayed. I don't know how I could have made it without you.

JANET: It wasn't me. You were so eager to learn about God. I was just there at the right time.

LYNNE: God put you there. Just like He put the star there 2,000 years ago. You were my personal star.

(They smile, but then laugh to break the embarrassed tension.)

JANET: Talk about stars, didn't I see you talking with Mary the other day?

LYNNE: She has so many hurts. She needs God in her life.

JANET: Well, I think God has led her to the right person.

LYNNE (looking up): I guess God has a new way of leading people to Jesus. Instead of shining light from heaven, He shines it through people.

JANET: And speaking of people, do you think they have sent out a search party yet?

LYNNE: Maybe we should go in. It's a bit nippy out here.

JANET: Sorry, it's too late. You'll have to come back for me in the spring. I'm frozen.

LYNNE: Come on. Maybe we can find some more of that hot apple cider.

JANET: Did you say hot! I think I can move for that.

(Fade as they exit. The group continues singing the hymn. Blackout.)